Redemption of Faith

Redemption of faith (My monologue series two)

Sailendra Nath Datta

PARTRIDGE
A Penguin Random House Company

To order additional copies of this book, contact
Partridge India
000 800 10062 62
orders.india@partridgepublishing.com

www.partridgepublishing.com/india

CONTENTS

To

All my well-wishers

Who had been and have

Been with me during my

Tortuous journey of life.

PREFACE

An offspring of Tagore—the first Nobel Laureate of Asia, in 1913, I have a philosophy somewhat akin to his. His idea of the 'god of life' was something unique, an idea which was at the same time simple and complex to comprehend, to grasp. But his faith in life and humanity— particularly life in the East and humanity in the West— was rather disturbed by the two World Wars as well as the socio-economic and political affairs and events in his domestic arena, i.e. India. Yet, his belief in the 'cosmic flow of joy' was integral to his poetic faith, the anchor to his philosophy. Despite the series of his personal loss in the family that he suffered during his long life, his public composure was like that of a Rishi, a saint. The 'Poet of the World', Rabindra Nath Tagore, was truly a cosmopolitan figure.

Similarly, my faith in life and humanity has often been shaken by the socio-economic troubles and travails of self and the mankind around that I've witnessed or known in the course of my career and life in general. I've been especially tormented by the abject poverty of the people, their struggle for basic needs of living, a frantic search for livelihood, the topical upheavals, the political ups and downs, and the unnecessary violence for partisan/political beliefs or gains, the illiteracy and superstitions prevalent in the common masses or their alarming ill-health, the caste system and the religious intolerance and so on. Some of these have been faithfully delineated in my previous book of poems, Resurrection of Pain.

Now also, imbued with Tagore's ideals and his example, it is through my fundamental optimism, my hope, my faith in the ultimate goodness of mankind that I've almost overcome the dark phase of my journey. Yet the struggle is still on. Like Tagore's, again, my stem of faith is in the simple belief that 'God is good', 'God is joy', 'God is gracious'! May Tagore's 'God of life' help me redeem my faith in humanity!

Kolkata, 8th. May, 2014

1) *Love and Faith*

Once I lost my olden love—
My love for troubled humanity.
That was a dark day for me
And I felt as shy as a dove.

When I lost my faith,
I thought I lost everything.
Be you a pauper or a king,
Faith holds you in life or death!

Then I tried heart and soul
To regain my lost feeling.
But it's too hard to find a lost thing
From the North to the South Pole.

My search for love would end
When it would be restored at last.
Faith rejuvenates you fast
And love helps your life extend.

~~~~~~ *04/09/13*

2) *Pain and Joy*

Every time my pain sinks.
My joy is renewed.
Every time my joy sinks,
My pain is reviewed.

It's like hide-and-seek—
It's like a child's game.
Pain makes you quite meek—
In joy, you have no fame.

If pain spurns my soul,
I feel rather lightened.
And if joy has its role,
Happiness is heightened.

When joy sinks, the pain floats—
And when pain sinks, joy bloats!

~   05/09/13

3) Hedonism is not your Goal

Hedonism is not your goal—
If you are a godly man!
Pleasure can't lift you up
As your philanthropic pains can.

Lord has His own measure
To judge your activity.
If you want to give him a slip,
You'll be caught in a pity.

When common man still suffers,
How can you seek happiness?
It's your duty to serve them—
In their sorrow and distress.

Don't aim to be mean and selfish,—
Lord loves them who fulfil his wish!

-- 05/09/13

4) Poetry was my first love

Once when I was
Mere twenty three,
I wished to live
Together with Poetry.

But life snatched me
Away from my beloved—
And I discovered
On a rainy day
That I was alone
In an empty bed.

Poetry was my first love
And she was my beloved.
Her separation was too heavy—
I felt lonely and deserted.

Now an old log as I am
And also tension-free,
I wish I'd find back
My fiancée Poetry !

--- --- --- --- --- --- --- --- --- --- --- --- --- --- --- --- --- --- 05/09/13

5) I am in the waiting room

I am in the waiting room—
Waiting for the arrival
Of the last express train
That would carry me
To the next junction
Of my terminal station.

The station master only
Knows if the train runs
On time or will be late—
I'm here waiting on my fate!

Hope the train will arrive
And depart on its schedule.
I have nothing to do but wait
Since all my daytime duties
Are already done in haste.

Now I'm waiting to hear
The whistle and see the signal
Of the last outgoing train
To the land of peace and calm.

~~~~~~ 05/09/13

6) *Sweetness goes with you*

All the sweetness
Goes with you, o dear!
And I deal with bitterness.

This is what is
Ordained for me, o dear!
And I deserve no less.

All the happiness
Is for you, o dear!
And I dwell in sadness.

This is what is
Fated for me, o dear!
And I carry on nonetheless.

06/09/13

7) *Love me once in a while*

I have ever been loyal
To you, oh my darling!
I have ever been faithful
To you all the while I'm living!

You have an aura of royal
Charm over you, oh darling!
And I have ever been meek
As a servant before a king.

Yet you do not look at me,
Look at me with a loving eye!
Is this my reward I deserve
Oh dear, for my sworn loyalty?

I beseech you, oh darling!
I beg you of a small favour—
Please love me once in a while
And ignore then as you think.

– 06/09/13

8) *Forgive me, oh my Master*

Forgive me, oh Lord of Life,
If ever I cannot carry out
Your given duty!

Forgive me, oh my Master,
If I turn away in neglect
From your divine beauty!

This earth, this world
And this big universe—
All praise you, oh Lord,
Through summers and winters.

I am the one, oh Lord,
Who lags behind them.
I forget to perform your task
And sing your anthem.

Forgive me, oh Lord, forgive
And bless me till I'm left to live!

~~~~~~ 07/09/13

9) *Let us part with sweet words*

No, no, no dear!
This is not any tear.
The drops ooze out
Because of a pain
In the core of my eyes
And not due to any
Ache in my heart.

Tell me, o sweetheart,
Why should I shed tears
In the joy of this union?

Maybe this will last
Only for a moment or two,
Maybe this will be
So short or transient!

Still there's no reason
For my tears to drop,
For my heart to weep. ——
Let us part with sweet words!

~~~~~~ 08/09/13

10) *Restore Love*

Life is so fast now,
Life is so hectic now
That people are insensible
And often forget to love.

People like me are insensitive to
What their dear ones feel.
People are quite insane to
What they need or want.

Couples no more love each other—
They do merely unite in sex!
This was not to have happened
If they transcend to be humans!

Love, the uniting bond, is lost;
Love, the blissful feeling, is missing.
Try hard to restore it back—
Since without love, there is nothing!

—————————————————————————————————— 08/09/13

11) *Our joys are tailor-made*

To live or not to live—
The decision is very tough.
Man has many problems here
And his means aren't enough.

Man's joys are tailor-made,
So are his customized sorrows.
There's someone who lends happiness
And someone who ever borrows.

To die or not to die early—
It's now a puzzle to one who is born.
Your dark night may not be as pleasant
As the sunshine-woven morn!

'Live and let live' is an old policy—
There are now few takers of it.
'Live and let die' is a better option
For those who are at the end of wit!

_   13/09/13

12) *Why is man still so unhappy?*

What is the fundamental truth about life?
And I wonder about the basics.
Is life only full of foul pains
And the sufferer needs analgesic!

Man has an illness that is ancient—
And so you may call it chronic.
He now suffers as no animals do,
Even through this age of electronics!

In this era of nano technology
Man can programme in a chip
The whole history of mankind,
But he can't solve the crypto quip
As to why man is still so unhappy!
Or, why is he still hungry and homeless?
These are quizzes that torment me
And make me cry in wilderness!

‑   *13/09/13*

13) The Saint has His love

Man has been perpetually banished
From the happy heaven above.
Yet he has been striving
For the restoration of love.

Man has been unduly greedy—
And disobedient to His command.
The Judge was quite pained at heart
To send him to the hellish remand.

Man lives by the sweat of his brow—
Still he hankers for the peace
That eludes him even for life,
And he remains devoid of the bliss.

The Judge only occasionally allows
His divine custody to a selected few,
Who pine for His love and abode.
Saints only bid the world adieu!

—   13/09/13

14) *Love is a Shower of light*

And God said, 'Let there be love',
And there was love.
For love is His light,
Love is His divine joy.

God doled out love
Among all His creatures.
He wanted everyone to share
His blissful gift of love.

But man has been ignorant,
Even intelligent though he is—
He has misused God's love
For cheap envy and malice.

Love illuminates every mind
As sunshine reveals the day.
So be aware of its light
And greet it like a shower.

- 13/09/13

15) *Every man is born of love*

If life is divorced from love
Or, love is divorced from life,
Man can no longer live
With his friend, son, or wife.

For, living a life without love
Is a very difficult proposition.
Even animals love their life
In the face of all opposition.

When relationship between people
Suddenly ends at a turn of life,
It becomes very hard to cope with
As lovelessness cuts like a knife.

Every man is born of love
And every man should die in love.
He shouldn't break the rule of life,
As ordained by his Lord from above.

17/09/13

16) *Let me revive my soul*

I've ever been in search of a thing
Like the purity of soul—
But this has eluded me ever
And makes me pine for my goal.

I might admit purity is an illusion—
Purity of love, or of friendship!
Man is now so business type
That he has no urge for relationship.

There are certain things in life
That you can't buy online.
Purity and integrity are two of them—
Those are too dear and divine.

I admit I don't any more find my soul—
Maybe it has been hibernating within,
Hibernating since I was a teenager.
Let me revive it from the frozen bin!

— 17/09/13

17) *I wish to die beside a stream*

Sometimes I feel an infatuation
Or, I feel a strong disposition
For a peaceful painless death
With a lifetime glory of wreath.

I wish to die by a gurgling stream
With my unfulfilled last dream—
Far from the everyday crowd,
With green foliage as a shroud.

I have a cherished desire to die
Under the canopy of an autumn sky,
When birds are heading for their nest
And the sun is reclining on the west.

I know this wish may seem so strange
Or, people may think I am deranged.
But truly speaking, it's my genuine wish—
Maybe, friend, it sounds quite boyish!

17/09/13

18) *War is nightmare*

Scarcely can I ever survive
From my nagging nightmare
Which very often would scare
Me to the bones and I strive
To get rid of the freezing horror
In a moment of hellish chill
And there's no savior except my will
That reflects in the hanging mirror.

The nightmare is all about war
That bullies inflict upon the weak
As if they try a fun to tweak
And make them tremble in terror.

Bullies hardly need an excuse
To wage an unequal battle
They kill others like the cattle
With impunity for the abuse!

~~~~~~ 17/09/13

19) *My footprints on the shore of life*

My footprints on the shore of life,
My footmarks on the shore of life
Will one day be erased out
By a sudden rushing wave.

I'll be taken into the lap of death,
I'll be seized into the lap of death
With no one there to mourn it,
Since I've left no indelible mark.

I've made no impact on the world,
I've made no imprint on the world
That recognizes us by our prints,
And by the way we impress it ever.

So, oft I wish to leave a stamp on stone,
So, oft I wish to keep a stamp on stone
That will be fossilized after I die,
And thus my friends will identify me!

— 22/09/13

20) *Winter melts into spring*

The sky-dome above spreads
A blue canopy overhead
And the golden ball of the sun
Sprinkles its spiky rays
To revive the frozen world
Into the vigorous activities
That are the definite signs
Of our terrestrial life on earth.

The pretty dome is gem-studded
In the clean beautiful night
With billions of twinkling stars
That illuminates the darkness.

Now winter melts into spring
That sprays its varied colours
Into the nature around us
For the rejuvenation of life!

--- 23/09/13

21) Man is the slave of systems

Now man is a slave of systems—
No more he obeys his heart
That's why he's so mechanical
And thus he plays his robotic part!

He speaks in a measured monotone,
He walks in a measured gait,
He eats in a civilized manner—
He is a modern man at any rate!

Man is seldom an individual
And he vies for unanimity.
Soon robots will produce man—
And that will be a big irony and pity!

A man is a man is a man—
So God made him in his shape.
But he wants to topple his creator,
Yet there's no way he can escape!

–   25/09/13

22) Many times I have been dead

Many times I have been dead
Before I am actually dying.
I know cowards die many times—
And it's so I am not lying.

Death is not the end of life—
So do the wise sages say.
Death is a new beginning for you
And you live by death any day.

I am not that wise, you know,
Or I don't believe in the role
I may play after my death
Through transmigration of soul.

I die many times in one life
As I am not so bold or brave.
Silence before tyranny is death—
And I'm dead ere I enter the grave!

- 28/09/13

23) Man is a cosmic wonder

We live as long as we breathe—
So the wise physicians would say.
But we continually writhe in pain
And may finish our existence soon
On one hot midsummer day.

We may be frozen on a May day
Or go into eternal hibernation
Like a total solar eclipse
On a nice unpredictable day.

Some people would again say
Your acts are predetermined
Like a fully programmed robot
That works on the commands
Stored in its brain till the end.
Man is a cosmic wonder
With no celestial parallel!

10/10/13

24) *Death is your last calamity*

Death is your last calamity,
Death is your final disaster—
If you can, however, overcome it
As you've done with some others,
You'll surely survive death and
Live a new life hereinafter.

What is death but a cessation
Of your terrestrial journey?
On a trip you came here alone and
Will also depart all by yourself!

What you see and do here on earth
Appears to be a fleeting dream.
As soon as you rise and ride on clouds,
Forget everything like a scripted film!

You live here in your own orbit
As every man does in his own orbit.

~~~~~~ *12/10/13*

25) Humanity is ailing

Mankind is still in great distress—
Thanks to wars or induced famine!
And not due to any natural calamities
That occasionally express their fury.

Humanity is ailing for long
And it needs a steady recovery.
Hunger brings about a slow death,
But intolerance or greed a huge toll.

I can't bear with a scenario where
Man decimates his fellow beings
For uncontrollable anger or avarice,
In his crooked and disguised mask!

Humanity is weeping for long
Ever since mankind's infancy.
It needs an empathetic healing—
No empty words or solace will do!

_____ 12/10/13

26) *Your inner soul has a discipline*

Your inner soul has a discipline——
It has a philosophy of its own.
If you lend an ear to listen,
You would certainly bemoan.

In most cases that you undergo
You don't follow its advices.
Virtues one's prone to overthrow
And tend to adhere to vices.

If you obey the dictates of mind,
You will certainly wonder to see
That those are nice and will find
A true guide in your mortal activity.

Your mind, inner self or soul
Is your real friend and philosopher.
So try to honour its given role
And the guidance it has to offer.

—— *12/10/13*

27) *Pain vibrates in me*

Pain throbs in me.
Pain vibrates in me.
My pain has a unique mass—
When unswollen, it weighs only
One-hundred-and-eighteen grams.

Bounded by hard walls of pity,
It only moves around
Within the prison of heart.
It can't wish away its existence!
The iron bars of the rib-cage
Are so strong that it cannot
Break away from the solitary cell.

Swollen by pride, it gains mass,
Swollen by tears, it gains mass.
It has got a unique character—
Condensed like balls of cream,
It never turns into a cold class.

My pain has a semi-solid density!

~~~~~~ *13/10/13*

28) *In the square of a cube*

Now that I've arrived
At the square of a cube,
I'm perfectly placed
Inside a dangling tube.

As I look back at
The history of the planet,
I have a vision of my journey
That often I would like to forget.

I remember I've come across
Many a womb through the past.
I may again travel in eons and
Reach the doors of eternity at last.

As the blue planet revolves
Round its solar parent,
I'm also moving along with it and
Soaring in open firmament.

————————————————————————————————————— 14/10/13

29) Be ready for the call of your heart

Whenever light
Kisses my eyelids,
I wake from slumber.
I am arisen not by time,
But by the touch of light.

Wait for the inner light
That glows and illuminates
Your sanctum sanctorum.
The saintly seer poet has
Rightly observed that
Daybreak doesn't come
At the end of night;
Morning happens
Whenever your heart awakens——
And then you start and go
To carry out your mission.

So, be ready
For the call of your heart
And plunge into your activity
As soon as your eyelids open,
Be it morn or midnight!

~~~~~~ 14/10/13

30) *A mother's departure*

That bundle of papers
Are very neatly filed.
And the file lies at the head side
Of our mother's empty bed.

It contains a description
Of mother's last nine days
In the special hospital,
With an account of her final
Treatment, medicines and so on.

Those are no longer of any use—
Such as the internal picture
Of mother's blocked head,
Or the nice digital mapping
Of her olden golden heart.
Everything now seems absurd!

It is clinically reported that
Both of mother's head and heart
Were too much damaged
By a fatal and final stroke.
We can't even now say if
All this information is correct.

But our mother had indeed
A prolonged pain in her chest
Since she received her first shock
When she became a young widow
And took charge of her children.

Yet the real reason of her death
(Our disregard and negligence),
Is strictly forbidden to be noted
In that thick roll of papers.

Now all of us here left on earth
Are looking for one thing—
One or two lines in short,
In the form of her legal
Death certificate, so that we,
Her non-bequeathed assets
Left behind, can scramble
Over her worldly property—
We are really waiting for that.
All other ordeals she had
Undergone are now meaningless.

Therefore the bundle of papers
Are still lying neatly filed
At our mother's bedside!

_   24/10/13

31) My Ancient sorrow

Plenty of tear has gathered,
Like a thick green phlegm
In my aerated lungs,
Inside my old ribcage.

Only at a soft touch
Of the Lord's feet
It turns into hot lava
And begins to erupt,
Choking my throat pipe.

An ancient sorrow
Has accumulated like
A green slime in the precinct
Of my heart, as on a flat
Platform of a pond's ghat.

Today the inevitable tsunami
Has washed away its every sign.
The sudden jolt of deluge
Has emptied my heart today!

————————————————————————————————— 24/10/13

32) *A song of inspiration*

Often I talk with the
Inner Lord who sits
Formless in the throne
Of my heart and also directs
Me to do or not to do things.
I, however, can't differentiate
Between what is good or bad!

Or, even if I know
The sin from the virtue,
I cannot perform
Or refrain accordingly.
And the invisible idol in me
Gets me follow His wish
According to divine scheme.

~~~~~~ 25/10/13

33) Have faith in the common man

Have faith in the common man—
Don't lose your trust in him.
He suffers most and yet he acts most
For your benefits and happiness.

The Lord has graciously endowed him
With the empathy for mankind—
Despite the fact that he may
Himself remain half-fed or hungry.

Humanity has a goal since beginning—
Be kind to others and try to be good.
Man should lift himself up
From generation to generation—
That's the basic difference
Between him and the wild animals!

~~~~~~~~~~~~~~~~~~~~~~~~~~~~~~~~~~~~~~ 25/10/13

34) An empty story

Let me tell you a simple story—
It gives you no lesson, nor worry.
You may call it an Everyman's Tale.
The scene may be a coast or a dale.

The plot is also quite easy—
None of the characters is too busy.
The time is any hour of the day,
Suppose in the month of March or May.

The events in it are commonplace—
As may happen to the human race.
And the climax is as you should hope.
For your comments, there is no scope.

The story isn't like a TV episode—
Or about a unique island abode.
It's a tale as you would imagine.
Is it so interestingly empty or thin?

~~~~~~ 25/10/13

35) A poem a day

A daily dose of a poem
Keeps me fit and well.
A daily gift of a sweet poem
Makes me happy as a bell.

When I read a good poem,
I feel quite recharged,
When I listen to a nice poem,
I fell very glad and purged.

When I happen to write a poem,
I think myself a winner.
The horizon widens for me—
The Muse alights for me to win her.

Because a good poem a day—
As I write or recite one,
Keeps all my ills away
And I feel a kingdom's won!

-- 27/10/13

36) *Do your own duty*

There are few auspicious moments
In the life of an ordinary man.
Those are set to clock and
Calendar by an invisible hand.

But you of course don't know
When such a moment will come.
So you need not wait for that
And finish your jobs at random.

Do your allotted duty in time.
See life is a series of tasks for you—
When you perform them well,
Your mission is complete and through.

Your Master takes notice of you
And so never lose your heart.
If you always do the right things,
He'll be pleased to play His part.

-- 27/10/13

37) *People still starve*

Peoples starve even in this
Two-do-fourteen, as they
Were used to two or twelve
Ancient centuries ago.
Some pundits would say
People indeed were indigent
Then, but now the economy
And history has changed a lot.
And today it is surely not
As true as of an earlier day.
Yet the plain fact remains so—
The poor is more poor
And hungrier now!

In all the continents
Of our dear planet
Social changes are of little use;
The increase of population
Does not matter much as do
The greed of the rich does.
Crops too now grow manifold
For all the people to feed.
But food is hoarded by them
And hunger or famine is doled.

REDEMPTION OF FAITH

The power-mongers usurp all and
The have-nots remain downtrodden,
As they did those long centuries ago!

——————————————————————————————————— *27/10/13*

38) *Nobody can Share agony.*

Nobody can actually share
Somebody else's agony.
And unsolicited sympathy
Increases the pain instead!

The sufferer only knows
Where the pain pinches.
The sympathizer only gropes
In darkness to find the root.

As the bereaved soul only knows
What the departed darling
Had been like to him and
What the loss really means!

The doleful person cannot be
Easily consoled and asked
To forget the cause of sorrow,
No matter you feel sad for them!

-   27/10/13

39) Man is selfish by nature

Man is selfish by nature—
All of them, at least
In their hidden mind.

Selfishness may vary in kind:
Money, power, fame or virtue—
Men may vie for one or the other.

Their struggle may be crude
Or, sometimes it's very subtle—
But the drive is ever the same.

Even service to God or mankind
May bring you to the limelight—
Self-interest is your bull's eye!

Selflessness is quite a rare thing
In this age of non-Samaritans!

~~~~~~ 27/10/13

40) *Our faith will redeem us*

Travelling like an aimless meteor
From one to the other worldly wish,
We're used to hanker for pleasure
And in the end receive anguish!

Someday will surely come
When we'll ascend from ourselves.
Someday will surely come
When we'll be lifted from ourselves!

Soaring through the seven heavens
We'll be resting for an aeon,
Before finally merging
With the supreme Halcyon.

Still we do however believe—
In the core of our hidden heart,
Our faith will one day redeem us
Before we prepare to depart!

~   30/10/13

41) *Over the dead leaves of pity*

When I watch an egg
Boiling in the pan,
My heart rolls and boils like it
As painfully as it can.

As the egg tosses in pain
Within its given field,
I think life's heat and pressure
Will similarly make me yield!

Under the chariot of Death-god
My egged heart is certain to burst,
Oozing drops of blood through
Every pore of my ancient thirst.

I'll be lying like a felled log
In the forest of humanity,
Five-feet seven inches tall—
Over the dead leaves of pity!

31/10/13

42) A cushion of pity

I fall upon the hard rock of life—
I'm shattered and go bleeding.
Life has been an arid plateau for me
That defies all my ardent pleading!

Life has been a dry and barren field,
Unirrigated by mercy or pity.
I am tossed like drops of ball and
Smashed into atoms of disintegrity.

What I need is the water of life,
But there's no hope for rejuvenating rain—
For my sky is devoid of clouds, and
What it pours is a shower of pain!

I know I am to suffer the wounds of life,
Whatever may be my propensity,
Life is so tough and unkind to me
That I urgently need a cushion of pity!

-   31/10/13

43) *Worldly hibernation*

Drawing a simile from
The sphere of journey by sea
On a long newfoundland trip,
I may wishfully say—
'Bon Voyage' to you,
'Happy Journey to you',
'Keep well' or 'May God bless you'!

On your solo tour abroad
To this land of emigration
With a terrestrial visa for
The life-long period you stay
There, as if in a dream sojourn,
You may well enjoy the illusion
Of being what you are not.

Or, drawing a simile from
Basic life as it is known to us,
I may again wistfully say—
You've been put on hibernation!

~   01/11/13

44) *I need some Space*

I need some space . . . some space—
I am tired of this daily rat race!

I'm tired of all those measured words
That are every day spoken towards
Me, or that I sometimes utter, in response
Which often ring like empty sermons.

I'm tired of hearing the hidden lies,
Tired of hearing the half-truth that flies
All around me in a dark circle
And allows no golden ray or sparkle
Of pure plain truth to penetrate it—
But, as an artificial man, I'm unfit!

Thus I'm tired of this rat race—
Of grinning and greeting each dark face!

Give me some space I badly need
Oh, my Life's Lord, please concede!

~~~~~~~~~~~~~~~~~~~~~~~~~~~~~~~~~~~~~~~ *04/11/13*

45) A plain sonnet to sadness

Oh, my sweet sadness,
You shall not go away,
Oh, my dear sadness—
I'll follow what you say.
Darling, only assure me
You won't leave me alone.
Please do stay with me,
As does flesh with bone.

I am in love with you,
Oh, my beloved sadness.
You're my old friend, not new—
Stay with me, oh sadness!
You are better than anybody,
So I plead you to stay with me!

~~~~~~~~~~~~~~~~~~~~~~~~~~~~~~~~~~~~~~~ 04/11/13

46) *Life is a different game*

Don't take everything for granted—
Life is a different game, oh dear!
Life is full of barbs and thorns,
Life is full of envy and scorns,
Life is full of worries and fear—
Never take all things for granted!

Once you might have been a darling don—
Fortune's most wanted person,
The most sought-after man, oh brother!
But the dice may soon change, rather,
Its old favourite man of the match—
To turn to a new Time-served catch!

So beware of this temporal game—
Life's a different scheme, a queer name!

~~~~~~ *04/11/13*

47) *Time is famous for disloyalty*

I've often been troubled
By the sweet betrayal of time!
I could not find any reason,
Nor I could find any rhyme!

Time is so famous for being
Disloyal to one whom he rejects!
Time is so fickle that he'd fret
Like an angry wasp which injects
Its liquid poison through soft tissue
Into the vulnerable human heart
That weeps and wails for its agony
Till the scheduled time to depart.

But all your troubles would only end
When you go to sleep, oh friend!
Yet that also depends upon the
Whims of time as he bleeps, oh friend!

~~~~~~~~~~~~~~~~~~~~~~~~~~~~~~~~~~~~~ 04/11/13

48) Malala, the miracle girl

Malala, Malala, you are our living faith!
Malala, Malala, you're our sworn belief
That everything is not yet lost,
That life still demands a big cost.

Malala, Malala, you are our commander!
Malala, Malala, you hold the torch for us
To enlighten the women world over,
To make the Peace-bird joyfully hover!

Malala, Malala, you're our torch bearer!
Malala, Malala, illuminate our dark path
That leads to empowerment and reason,
That widens our daily human horizon.

Malala, Malala, you are an icon of this Age!
Malala, Malala, you'd bring about a miracle
To cleanse the debris of suppression,
To spread the message of education!

~~~~~~   04/11/13

49) My tryst with life is uncertain

My tryst with life is uncertain.
My present tryst with life
Is nearing the fifth act last scene
And the final fall of the curtain!

At the end of the current play
Or, the end-game, as you may
Call the final stage at its best,
The players would go for a rest.

The ultimate leisure is a matter
Of great comfort and peace
For the act-fatigued actor so
Passively prompted by the lease.

The actor is now in a reverie
Dreaming for a fresh tryst
With another unknown beloved
In an unknown land of mist!

-- 04/11/13

61

50) Sorrow is pandemic

Sorrow is essentially pandemic.
It spreads like a cold morning mist
And wraps everything in view.
My sorrow is quite deep and thick.

My sorrow often engulfs my mind,
My sorrow shrouds my sad memory.
I am lost in the dense fog of sorrow
And so seek sunshine for mankind.

Mankind is sunk deep in depravity—
Life's basic needs are seldom fulfilled,
Even when sham progress touches
Mars, outwitting the rules of gravity.

It's a shame man sends Curiosity
To the red planet to see how it is,
While he's not curious to know how
His brothers die for the lack of pity!

~~~~~~~~~~~~~~~~~~~~~~~~~~~~~~~~~~~~~~~ 04/11/13

51) *Journey of sunshine*

Sunshine from the waking east
Falls on the shivering dewdrops,
Atop the morning blades of grass;
And sparkles of tiny diamonds
Glitter like a vibrant necklace!

Sunshine from the tiring west
Enters my living room in a slant
And leans wearily on my bed.
Sunshine gradually turns its life into
Sprays of dusk red on the horizon.

I like this daily pleasant journey
Of the sunshine from dawn to dusk
Across the dreary path of my day
Till it vanishes behind the skyline!

~~~~~~ 05/11/13

52) *Bid me an early farewell*

Let me bid adieu, oh my Friend!
Let me bid adieu, oh my Host!
I spent my joyous time at your place
As a very dear and chosen guest—
Now, let me take my journey to the west!

I've enjoyed my brief stay at your place
Now I am to complete my sojourn soon.
So let me bid farewell with a smile
And follow my itinerary at its best.

At this sudden unplanned departure
What I can give you is a glittering
Bouquet of flowers that you may hold
In a vase of sad memory which would
Fade over the years like the incense
Of a slow-burning heart that emits an
Unfamiliar sweet fragrance in the air!

~~~~~~ *06/11/13*

53) I'll be crash-landing one day

When my problem turns red,
I know it's going to be a danger.
When my crisis turns to be violet,
I know a violent storm is brewing on.

A black hole will seldom change its hue—
It swallows everything, and even light.
It engulfs my whole existence and fate,
And I am one with the endless night.

It is quite rare my sky turns blue
Or lets golden light through its pores.
My orbit of life is so elliptical
That it defies every ray of hope.

Troubles of livelihood rob my vitality
And I'm left to rotate around death.
If my centrifugal force lessens one day,
I'll be crash-landing with no harm control!

_   11/11/13

54) Build Life with bricks of faith

Life has sorrows, we know,
And life has pains.
Yet life has tranquil peace
When it feeds on our faith.

As life rolls on,
It touches many harbours
On its way of shipping.
Only a few lighthouses are
There to guide you to safety.

There are pitfalls and vortex
Which the sailor should best avoid
While sailing quite unmindfully.
You may again break your route
And your trip may come to an end.

You need to have faith in yourself
And build your life with its bricks!

~~~~~~~~~~~~~~~~~~~~~~~~~~~~~~~~~~~~~~~ 19/11/13

55) *I have a sleeping conscience*

I am daily tormented
By the loss of humanity.
Lots of hunger, sickness,
Illiteracy, ill-health and more
Daily cripple its structure.

Every day I go on neglecting
The sorrows and sufferings of man
Who lives next door, and ignore
The pangs of my inner soul,
Thanks to my own dear status!

I subscribe to the fond view
That luck has been on my side
Or, I've achieved things on my own.
But the high economist knows well
That every man is a sum of others.

So my daily agony is meaningless—
It's an excuse for the sleeping
Conscience that still hibernates!

~   20/11/13

56) Something is wrong with time

Something is wrong with my time——
Something is wrong with everybody,
I think something is wrong with me, too!
I think time aches from a bad carbuncle.

It's so strange time never counts his days,
For his days are never numbered.
Yet he now has to count his pain——
Such a bad patch has come in his life!

Men like me seem to be content——
They think they've done their duty.
It is the lot given to the downtrodden
That they quite often starve or suffer!

Time is as old as the cosmos, you know.
Maybe he's made from a monolith.
Yet he is so inane to the mankind
That he bothers little about their pith!

_   22/11/13

57) God is my vital Spirit

Now that you know God particle is
Omnipresent throughout the universe,
You should not disbelieve His existence
In everything that you see around you.

You should not ever argue that
Things are blessed with His creative joy,
That things owe their weight and
Gravity to His invisible grace.

Divinity permeates all things He created—
A cosmic plan pre-exists every phenomenon.
Man is no exception to this divine rule,
Sure he has an unlimited potential!

I often shiver to the core of my soul
Whenever I think that God dwells in me,
That He is in the temple of my body—
That he's ever awake as my vital spirit!

--------------------------------------- 25/11/13

58) *Flames of desire*

Man has many a desire—
Some of which are fulfilled
And some are cast away.

Man lives for a series of desires,
Which are renewed one by one.——
Pleasure or happiness is his goal.

But man doesn't make his fortune!
He is ignorant about tomorrow;
Unpredictability is his dear fate.

One thirst isn't quenched by another—
So let your desire be limited,
If peace in life is your sole aim.

Flames of desire won't cool you down.
Let all happiness spring from the heart!

29/11/13

59) I am fond of pains

I have a liking for small pains—
They are better and more loyal
To me ever since my boyhood
Than the big pleasures so rare!

That's why I like the faithful pains—
As they stay with me in weal and woe.
Pleasures only seek for a merry wind
That blows infrequently over my horizon.

I'm really fond of my favourite pains—
They seldom fail me in bad crisis.
But pleasures often look for a mood
If they prefer to give me company!

Yet I have a preference for pains
That emit their familiar smell,
While I remain afraid of pleasures
That hypnotize me with a lulling spell!

-- 01/12/13

60) Fill in more light

Fill in more light,
More light into my eyes,
Oh, my Lord of life!
So that I can see
Everything brighter—
The green forest
And the blue skies!

Fill in more light
And illuminate
My dark interior,
So that your seat
In the inner temple
Looks shiny and bright
And I don't feel,
I never feel inferior.

Fill in more light,
Lord! Be kind to me,
So that everything
Comes within my sight
And I can serve others
Truly and quite humbly!

03/12/13

61) I've come for a short visit

I've come for a short visit
To your place here by the woods.
I won't stay for any longer
Than you would kindly permit.

And I have no other plans than
To see you for a few moments,
To have a few words of courtesy
And then leave as silently as I can.

Or, if you even don't like so,
I would go back without a noise
After I watch your sweet face from
A hiding through the window.

For I know nothing more happens
Than God has ordained for me.
If our union is denied by Fate,
It's not likely that your heart opens!

~~~~~~~~~~~~~~~~~~~~~~~~~~~~~~~~~~~~~~ 03/12/13

62) What is yours is yours

The portion that is yours
Belongs to you—
Nothing more, nothing less.
You cannot claim more,
Or you cannot have more.

If you have something more,
That will be shed and lost.
If you have something less,
Master knows how you will
Gain it through gift or miracle.

You may call it fortune
Or, you may name it fate.
But what is yours is yours—
Everything is predetermined,
Ever since before you're born
And till the time you are ashes!

- 05/12/13

63) My dear world

I am amazed by the
Pied beauty of the world—
I am amazed by the
Splendid light of the sun,
The moon or the auroras.
I am amazed by the
Water colours of the lake,
The brook or the ocean.

I am amazed by the
Shapes, sizes and designs
Of the myriads of leaves,
Flowers and fruits of the world.
I am amazed by the
Endless variety of birds,
Butterflies and animals that
Showcase our blue planet.

I am amazed by the
Forests and mountains.
I am amazed by the
Clouds and hues of the sky.

So all my thanks go to Him
Who's created all this
Beautiful world I can see
And I am living in!

07/12/13

64) I want to be sunshine

I want to be sunshine
And spread across the space
To fall on the every nook
Of this pretty dear earth.
I want to illuminate
Every grove or hill or home.

I want to carry the message
From heavens and scatter it
Through my cluster of beams
To enlighten every human heart.

I want to be sunshine
And light up the dark corners of
The world where mankind dwells
In the morning of fulfillment.

~~~~~~~~~~~~~~~~~~~~~~~~~~~~~~~~~~~~~~ 08/12/13

65) *Grief is my hallmark*

Grief is my heart's hallmark—
It is my level of purity.
Happiness is an antithesis
Of sorrow, and I always
Look for human dignity.

My sadness is the crystal
Of a gem that I value
Above all the diamonds.
Dejection always ignites
Your soul and is sure to
Build up human bonds.

Mankind is a long chain
Of individuals like the
Necklace with many a gem—
And there is ever a strong
Heart-to-heart link which
Hardly people condemn.

The human spirit only is
Immortal and it transcends from
One generation to another.
Grief is a guiding force
For the lasting spirit that
Binds a man to his brother.

~~~~~~ 08/12/13

66) Your temple is everywhere

Oh, Lord of the world!
Your temple is everywhere!
Yet I cannot see it,
Although I am very near.

You dwell in every tree,
In every animal or bird.
But I search in vain,
Here and there quite hard.

You dwell in every man,
On the altar of his heart.
Yet I seek you out as the blind
And forget my divine part.

Oh, my Lord of the world!
Lead me to the light,
So that I do find you anywhere
With your blessed insight.

~~~~~~~~~~~~~~~~~~~~~~~~~~~~~~~~~~~~~~ 08/12/13

67) Image and true self

I am what I am.
If I brag more,
Then I am sham!

If I zoom less,
That's not the truth—
I falsely profess!

Looks often deceive
And hide the true self
From what we receive!

Most men are thus
Who show a false face—
As if in a circus!

Mirrors too distort
What you see in front—
So, waste no effort!

- 18/12/13

68) *You need not be too clever*

As soon as you are happy,
You've reached the dead end.
You can't return to unhappiness—
Your journey you can't extend!

So I oft fail to understand
What does happiness mean!
All happiness is transitory and
We return to where we'd been!

Happiness is not the real goal—
What you need is surge ahead.
No matter you're happy or sad,
Make sure you're graciously led.

As we try to make living an art
And breathe in fresh energy ever,
Our life will surely be fulfilled
If we don't wish to be too clever!

~ 18/12/13

69) *Please don't forget me*

Why can't I depend upon you,
Oh, my eternal Master?
Why can't I surrender
Myself to your wish,
Oh, my infinite Master?

Since I know
My Lord is good,
Since I know
My Lord has been good,
Since I know
My Lord will ever be good,
Since I know
My Lord is just and kind,
Why do still I need
An excuse to have my trust
In you, oh, my Master?

Why do I behave like
A fallen unbeliever,
A common unbeliever
In my daily offerings
Of the ailing heart?
Why do I fail to listen to
The dictates of my soul
And aimlessly wander like
A born vagabond,
Oh, my limitless Master?

While you are ever there—
The source of all the riches,
The source of real wealth,
The source of all the peace?

You, therefore, need not
Forgive me just now,
Oh, my everlasting Master!
But please don't forget me!

_20/12/13_

70) *I dwell in you, oh Lord!*

I dwell in you, oh my Lord!
You are my ultimate home.
I do wander, I do stray—
But once I'll return to you!

I am like a small child
Who likes to waddle within
The four walls of his room and
Finally jumps into mother's arms.

I am like a small child
Who likes to babble about
Whatever he has seen and
Has felt all the day.

But in the evening he is very quiet;
He is calm and pleasantly silent.
I also want to have my last shelter
In your peaceful house, oh Lord!

~~~~~~~~~~~~~~~~~~~~~~~~~~~~~~~~~~~~~ *20/12/13*

71) Had I been a bit more fool

I've been a bit too shrewd
Oh Lord, I've not been frank.
I guess I've been a bit crude—
God knows it's your own prank!

You want to play hide and seek
With me, a poor helpless boy.
I wish I could have been so meek
That you won't use me like a toy!

If I had been a puppet for you,
The string ever remains in your hand.
You have your own tricks, old and new,
To openly cheer me or reprimand!

Now I wish I were a bit more fool
So that you'd have loved me more.
I know the game ever follows your rule
Even if it makes me sad or sore!

~   20/12/13

72) *Remove my stains*

My robe is full of stains—
There are marks of sorrows;
There is the stamp of pains.

It bears the signs of struggle
Over my age-old wearied heart.
It carries the stamp of burden
That distorts my appearance.

Wash away the dirt of mind
And cleanse me of the dust
That soil my identity, oh Lord!

Remove the stains that look like rust
And make my robe all clean and smart.
Replace my pains, oh dear Lord,
With your ever-fluent blessing!

–––   23/12/13

73) My new year is painful

My new year comes
On the trail of the old,
That has often been bitter
And has seldom been gold.

Every New Year comes naturally
At the end of the old calendar—
With each day changing the date
And making me one year older.

My new year comes around
When my planet completes its trip
Round my sun on its axis and orbit,
With olden faith and fresh friendship.

My new year repeats the sorrow
That I bear for the mankind.
It suffers and gives me pain
As I look disdainfully behind!

- 01/01/14

74) Memories mark moments

Do memories mark moments
Or moments make memories?
Sometimes I'm in a fix to decide
Which is real of the two stories!

My memories fade over the years
And moments are lost in eternity.
Although I try to retrieve some of them,
It's futile and it's a pity!

It's hide-and-seek between memory
And oblivion, when bubbling memories
Float over soon-to-vanish moments
Or, when my deep and heavy moments
Sink in everlasting dream-like memory—
An unrest within my entity foments.

There are some monumental moments
In everybody's birth-to-death existence.
They show off like iconic emblems,
While most memories die without pretence!

~~~~~~ 02/01/14

75) Common man's everyday song

I am an ordinary man and
I belong to the Common Man's Party
But I ever remain invisible and unknown—
I remain half-fed, half-clad and dirty.

I've always been a common man,
But I am not common with the others.
I'm a victim of hate and disdain—
Since I have no rich sisters or brothers.

Common Man isn't not my real identity—
It's a misnomer for people like me.
For, we share nothing in common,
Except human blood or human body.

We differ even in hunger or anger,
Because we ever remain hungry.
Better they call us Ordinary Man,
The fellows who seldom get angry!

~~~~~~~~~~~~~~~~~~~~~~~~~~~~~~~~~~~~~~ 05/01/14

76) A half-sonnet on mind

Every young mind takes to poetry—
Every young mind is essentially poetic,
Every young mind is basically romantic.

And minds can ever remain young—
Minds can ever remain to be fresh,
Minds can endure strain and stress.

Once upon a time I had a young mind—
But with fading days it grew weak and old,
With passing time it's no more that bold.

I don't know if every mind is so fated—
I don't know if it ever happens to be,
As it has painfully happened with me.

I can't say if the mind withers like a flower
And finally drops from the bliss of bower!

~~~~~~ 10/01/14

77) A few lines on my old heart

My heart beep-beeps
With its every beat.
It reminds me often that
My solitary heart
Seldom keeps
Pace with cardiac art.

It also tells me again
That everything is not right.
It tells me that
Life is in great pain.

Life is good risk
Since my erratic heart
Has never been so strong.
It struggles alone to breathe
And so would soon depart,
Lest pains make me writhe.

Although it's a great feat
That my personal heart
Has carried me on so long
Without any bad effort.

Now the North wind is so brisk
And the sun is neither bright.
Let me draw into the shell
And wait for the final bell!

——————————————————————————————————— 12/01/14

78) She is my unfound love

She is as tall as my heart,
She is as deep as my memory.
She is my living part,
She is my ancient story.

She is as wide as the sea,
She is as distant as the sky.
She is as sweet as honey,
She is my happy butterfly.

She is as pretty as a nymph,
She is as good as a holy idol.
She is as sacred as a hymn,
She is whom I adore and call.

She is as pure as my wish,
She dwells in the heaven above.
She is my divine joy and anguish,
She is my ever-unfound love!

--- 16/01/14

79) I'll redeem my soul

My soul, my soul,
I've mortgaged you to fear—
I've mortgaged you
To the fear of violence
And to the fear of death!

But, my soul, you are
Above the arena of death—
You are the idol of the Lord
Who is my almighty.

As I am, oh Lord, ever prone
To the fear of my silence,
Please whip me not to any length—
Pity incarnate as you are!

My soul, oh my kind soul,
Please forgive me, oh Lord!
Shower your blissful mercy
Upon me and give me strength.

My soul, my soul,
I'll certainly redeem you
From the mortgage to fear
And restore you to the throne!

--------------------------------------- *24/01/14*

80) Eyes reflect our mind

Your eyes reflect your mind—
If we delve deep, we'll find
Your various emotions and moods—
Now it echoes joy, now it broods.

Eyes are the mirror of your heart,
And faithfully play their given part.
They reflect your happiness and sorrow,
Not of yesterday, nor of tomorrow.

Eyes are the index of your soul.
They sometimes betray its divine role,
Be you in a mood, joyous or sad!
Or, you feel blessed or feel bad.

Eyes are your perfect looking glass
That makes you look your own class.
They do paint an inner image—
Be they blue, black, green or beige!

----------------------------------- 29/01/14

81) One life is not enough

Only once is not enough—
Only one life is not enough.
You cannot fulfil all your wishes
In one life, so full of wishes!

I wish to live a thousand years,
Or be reborn every forty years—
To see how the life changes,
To enjoy the way life changes!

The unresolved wishes may return—
In every new life the cycle would return.
My life may serially progress,
As do the linked TV episodes progress!

So one given life is not enough—
My allotted time must be long enough,
So that I can walk my full road—
My Desire Boulevard, my dream road!

~   29/01/14

82) The supreme time vendor

There is a supreme time vendor
Who dwells quite high above us,
And he vends different sizes
Or shapes of time for each of us.

His vending machine is eternally on,
That doles out time to poor folk.
There is a slot for every given time—
Whatever moods it may evoke!

You may be sad
Or, you may be glad
With the slice of time you get—
They name and call it your fate!

But the vendor is ever happy—
He's not moved by any mood.
You may be right or wrong,
Yet the vendor is always good!

‒   30/01/14

83) *Keep me fit, oh Lord!*

Keep me fit, oh Lord,
Keep me ever fit,
So that I can stand the storm
To its worst limit.

You've given me life
And as long as you let me live,
Give me strength, oh Lord,
Please continue to give!

You may give me other things—
You may give me great sorrow.
But please make it sure
That I can bear it till tomorrow!

I may live only until today
Or, I may die any moment.
But I'll be obliged much
If you're kind, oh Omnipotent!

-- 06/02/14

84) Man is not his mirror image

Sometimes I jest at myself,
Sometimes I like to make faces
At me on the looking glass
And want to see how ugly I am!

Every man has an ugly self
Of which he is seldom aware.
And it plays hide-and-seek
With the gentleman that shows.

Man isn't a mirror image he looks—
He may hide so much pain and sorrow,
And so much shame and melancholy—
That has been his part and parcel.

Therefore I sometimes try to make
Some malignant jokes with me
That may harm hidden ugliness
And my image may look brighter.

--------------------------------------- 08/02/14

85) All first things are great

The first love letter is
Very timid and hesitant.
It takes quite a long time
And effort to complete it.

The first flight of a nestling
Has to wait long before
Its wings strong and bold
Enough to dare the vast sky.

Parents need to be patient
Before they can hear the
First broken words of the baby
Who toddle down the room.

The first kiss is the sweetest
But rather half-hearted and
Quite shaken and unsteady.
All first things are so great!

~~~~~~ 08/02/14

86) Cancer spreads furtively

Cancer is a deadly disease.——
If you carry it in your womb
Or, develop it to the final stage,
It can surely bring you to the tomb.

Cancer needs a period of gestation,
To damage or kill the cells of life.
If one is vulnerable to its tentacles,
The crab slices him like a knife.

Society has a few pockets of cancer
That grows and develops furtively.
The tissues become quite malignant
And need surgery to be done curatively.

But the team of surgeons waver—
They hesitate to take drastic measure.
And the disease spreads far and wide
Without any fear and with pleasure.

~~~~~~ 09/02/14

87) Time travels westward

Don't waste your time,
Friend, please don't waste!
For, time travels fast
From the east to the west.
And there's no guarantee
It will again reach the east
Going around the night.

You don't know either,
You don't know whether
The night is dark or bright,
Whether it's a disc or a sickle.

The night is rather sickly—
It indulges all sickness,
All black or dark things
To grow and thrive
Within its dark womb.

And a day is a day—
Even if gloomy or gay.
It has its own light,
That may be the best
Depending upon its great
Lord of the seven horses.

So run with the day,
Run with your best time
And rest with the night,
Your last sleeping bag.

Count all your joys and
Forget all the remorses.
Your east welcomes you and
The west bids adieu at last,
To invite you into the tomb
Where darkness wraps you
And you are excused of
Your sordid mind eternally!

88) Clean my impurities, oh Lord!

Let me reduce the garbage
Of life, oh my Lord!
I've accumulated so much
Filth— dirt and dust
Throughout my past life
That I cannot clean it now.

Now that I'm going to diminish
All the unnecessary, smelling
Heaps and piles of rubbish
That has covered my heavenly
Horizon and hid me
From your graceful view,
Cleanse me of all this, oh Lord!

You are merciful, oh Lord!
You are so kind and gracious!
And I've been living as a blind!
I can't see your divine light—
Please excuse me, forgive me
For my childish ignorance.
Give me unwavering faith
And lift me up beside you!